10306862

Visit us on the web at:
www.alta.lib.ia.us
or call (712) 200-1250
to renew your books!

Like us on
Facebook

Careers in Construction

Carpenter

Cathleen Small

Cavendish
Square

New York

Published in 2016 by Cavendish Square Publishing, LLC
243 5th Avenue, Suite 136, New York, NY 10016

Cataloging-in-Publication Data

Small, Cathleen.
Carpenter / by Cathleen Small.
p. cm. — (Careers in construction)
Includes index.
ISBN 978-1-5026-0984-7 (hardcover) ISBN 978-1-5026-0985-4 (ebook)
1. Carpentry — Vocational guidance — Juvenile literature. 2. Carpenters — Juvenile literature.
I. Small, Cathleen. II. Title.
TH5608.7 S63 2016
694'.023'73—d23

Editorial Director: David McNamara
Editor: Andrew Coddington, Kelly Spence
Copy Editor: Rebecca Rohan
Art Director: Jeffrey Talbot
Designer: Alan Sliwinski
Senior Production Manager: Jennifer Ryder-Talbot
Production Editor: Renni Johnson
Photo Research: J8 Media

The photographs in this book are used by permission and through the courtesy of: sculpies/Shutterstock.com, cover; Scratch Video/Shutterstock.com, 4; cappi thompson/Shutterstock.com, 8; khuang54/iStock/Thinkstock, 10; Photos.com/PHOTOS.com/Thinkstock, 14; Katherine Frey/The Washington Post via Getty Images, 18; Ken Hively/Los Angeles Times via Getty Images, 20; OLI SCARFF/AFP/Getty Images, 21; aastock/Shutterstock.com, 30; © iStock.com/LanaDjuric, 33; DeAgostini/Getty Images, 35; image courtesy of Tyler FuQua, 36; image courtesy of Tyler FuQua, 38; image courtesy of Tyler FuQua, 39; Monkey Business Images/Shutterstock.com, 42; Goodluz/Shutterstock.com, 49; Vadim Ratnikov/Shutterstock.com, 54; bikeriderlondon/Shutterstock.com, 58; viki2win/Shutterstock.com, 60; Jesus Cervantes/Shutterstock.com, 62; Balefire/Shutterstock.com, 63; © iStock.com/gimages777, 64; Smokedsalmon/Shutterstock.com, 66; © iStock.com/baranozdemir, 67; thieury/Shutterstock.com, 70; © iStock.com/Steve Debenport, 72; © iStock.com/franckreporter, 75; luckyraccoon/Shutterstock.com, 78; Felix Lipov/Shutterstock.com, 80; Carlos gpointstudio/Shutterstock.com, 85 The LIFE Picture Collection/Getty Images, 88; Tyler Olson/Shutterstock.com, 99.

Printed in the United States of America

Table of Contents

Ancient cave dwellings located in Petra, Jordan

Introduction

Look around. You will see that you are literally surrounded by the work of highly skilled employees in the field of construction. An electrician would have run the wiring that carries light throughout your home, and the pipes that bring water to and from your house would have been installed by a plumber. If you look even closer, you will see the work of carpenters everywhere: in the frame of a wall, the decorative moldings of a hotel lobby, and even in the desk you sit in at school.

Technically speaking, the field of carpentry has been around for thousands of years. Even before the invention of tools, humans fashioned crude dwellings and structures to live in out of caves, rocks, and, in some parts of the world, ice and snow. Once humans evolved and began to make and use tools, the field of carpentry became more like what we know it as today—people using tools and building materials to construct dwellings, structures, and devices needed for daily life.

The carpentry field grew largely out of necessity. Long ago, men built shelter and furniture for their own families, but eventually there became a growing need for dedicated people to build pieces and structures for other purposes as well. Public buildings were needed in towns and villages, including places of worship, such as churches and temples. People needed furniture to fill those buildings, bridges to cross rivers, and so on. The men who practiced this craft became known as carpenters.

Carpentry is a trade. Learning a trade involves mastering the skills of a specific manual or technical job. People who work in these types of jobs are also known as tradespeople. In construction projects, many skilled tradespeople are needed to put together the various parts. A building project in particular often begins with an architect's vision. It is the skilled workers, like carpenters, who bring that vision to life. It takes these talented people working as a team to construct anything, from a towering skyscraper to a residential home.

Carpenters are involved during most stages of a project. Rough carpentry takes place early and usually involves the framing of a structure like a house, tunnel, or bridge. While this work is not visible in the finished product, it provides a safe and solid foundation for the work that follows. Finish carpentry involves adding the final details to a project, such as installing doors, cabinets, or moldings.

What makes carpentry an exciting field is the changes in design and technology that keep it fresh and revitalized. To get a better idea of this, study photos of houses from different decades. For example, look at a kitchen from the turn of the twentieth century and compare it to one from the 1950s, when the midcentury modern design aesthetic was popular. The finishes—the cabinets, the counters, the floors, the baseboards, the windows—look very different. Then, look at a picture of a kitchen from the 1980s. Different again! Take a look around at the modern kitchens we see today. Different still! Often designers will incorporate elements that are reminiscent of a past design sensibility, such as incorporating a vintage refrigerator into an otherwise modern and elegant kitchen, but the look is never quite the same. Carpenters who work on these finishes are constantly evolving and refining the style of their work.

Traditionally, carpenters are involved in two kinds of projects: new construction or remodels. New construction includes brand-new projects where everything is started from scratch, such as building a townhouse in a subdivision. A remodel involves the renovation of parts, or all of, a residential or commercial building. Although each project has distinct needs, carpenters require many of the same skills to work remodels and new builds.

Whether a carpenter is working on a new build or a remodel, correct measurements are key to any building project.

In addition, changes in technology ensure that carpenters learn new techniques throughout their career, even though they're technically doing the same basic tasks they have been doing for thousands of years. The cabinetmaker of today is certainly using different tools and technologies to build cabinets than the cabinetmakers of the thirteen original colonies did, but they're both accomplishing the same goal: building cabinets. One did it by hand and with no electricity, and the other likely used power tools to accomplish the same thing much more quickly and precisely!

Carpentry is a steadily growing, essential part of the construction industry. Carpenters who effectively combine the artistic sensibility and the scientific knowledge needed to master their craft are respected for their skill and dedication. If you enjoy taking pride in a completed project and working with your hands, then a career in carpentry may be a great fit for you.

The Nanchan Temple in China is one of the oldest structures in the world.

CHAPTER 1

The History of Carpentry

Carpentry may be one of the oldest occupations, dating back to prehistoric times. In Germany, evidence of early carpentry has been discovered dating back approximately seven thousand years to the early **Neolithic** period. In 2012, four wooden water wells that appear to have been built between 5600 and 4900 BCE were discovered near Leipzig, Germany. The wells were made of oak and were remarkably well preserved for their age, due to being **hermetically** sealed below sea level. Each well was made out of oak trunks that were cut to length through charring in a fire. Once all the pieces were the necessary length, they were joined together in a square shape. These wells were likely built by farmers and demonstrate early carpentry skills and surprisingly advanced construction techniques.

What's in a Name?

The word *carpenter* comes from the Old French word *carpentier*. This was in turn derived from the Latin word *carpentrius*, which means "maker of a carriage." These days, a carpenter might make a carriage, but they work on a lot of other projects, too, such as houses, buildings, bridges, ships, and furniture. A similar word in Middle English was *wright* (from the Old English *wryhta*), which basically means "builder." It was often combined with another word to identify a specialty craftsman, such as a *millwright*, who works with machinery, or a *wheelwright*, who builds and repairs wheels.

One of the earliest building materials to be used was wood. In many regions it was abundant, easily harvested, and relatively easy to work with. Think about it: birds use twigs to build nests, and beavers use wood to build dams. It probably didn't take too long for humans to realize that they, too, could use wood to build shelter.

For a long time, carpenters primarily worked with wood. It was plentiful, and the tools created during the Stone, Bronze, and Iron Ages made it easy to fashion nearly any structure out of wood. Wood was relatively durable, too, and is generally able to stand up against wear and tear from time and weather. A few wooden churches dating as far back as the eleventh to thirteenth centuries still exist, and an ancient wooden Chinese temple built in 782 CE still stands today.

The simplest log cabins required homebuilders to find logs and hew, or chop, the notches necessary to fit the logs together at the ends. (Think of the Lincoln Logs you may have played with as a child.) As time went on, however, humans began to desire more than just simple, crude structures. They began to cut and shape wood into planks and boards to provide more flexibility in how they could fashion their buildings. They also began to use wood to build furniture such as beds, tables, and chairs.

The invention of the sawmill, which dates back to the third century, furthered the use of lumber as a common building material. Once a log arrived at the sawmill, the bark was stripped, and the logs were shaped into planks of lumber. Sawmills became increasingly common in Europe as the Middle Ages progressed, and when the United States was first colonized, sawmills were quickly introduced so the colonists could build the homes and other structures needed to settle new towns. In many areas there was no need to look further than the forest for building materials—trees were plentiful, sawmills made

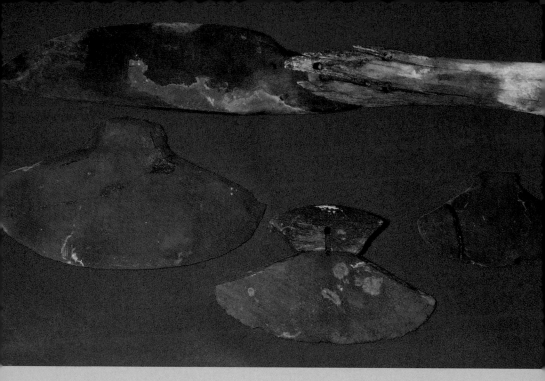

When primitive tools made out of stone and wood were invented, the field of carpentry advanced.

creating lumber a relatively easy task, and carpenters knew how to work with wood. This knowledge and craft was passed down from one generation to the next.

Learning the Trade

Before written language was invented, carpenters passed their skills on to the next generation orally, similar to an **apprenticeship** today. For example, a father might pass his knowledge of carpentry on to his son when his son came of age. Written records of architecture were few at this time. The Roman architect Vitruvius wrote his book *De architectura* (also known as *Ten Books on Architecture)* in about 15 BCE. The book remains the oldest known publication on architecture and an important source of information about Roman design and building methods. It contains information about carpentry in the Roman era and was particularly influential during the Middle Ages and the Renaissance.

After the printing press was invented, carpentry knowledge and practices could be recorded in books and manuals. This became common practice in the eighteenth and nineteenth centuries. Now, people who weren't directly related to a carpenter could also learn the trade if they desired.

Today, although books and manuals on carpentry are plentiful and available both in print and electronically, there remains no substitute for hands-on training in the field. Carpentry is a manual profession, so while books and printed materials are an excellent resource, they work best when paired with hands-on training.

Carpentry Today

Although many think of carpenters as being people who build things with wood, in reality wood is just *one* of the materials a carpenter can work with.

Eventually, architects and carpenters began experimenting with new kinds of building materials, such as brick, concrete, stucco, drywall, and plywood.

THE MOST FAMOUS CARPENTER

In general, carpenters aren't the rock stars of any era: their names aren't particularly well known, and they aren't chased down the street by paparazzi dying for a picture. But there is one carpenter whose name is very well known: Jesus. Regardless of one's religious beliefs, virtually all modern scholars of antiquity agree that a man named Jesus did exist, and many agree that he was a carpenter (although some say he was a stonemason and some say a handyman, not a carpenter). Those who are not convinced he was a carpenter do believe that his adoptive father, Joseph, was indeed a carpenter, so clearly the profession existed in Jesus's time—even if it remains a mystery as to whether Jesus himself was a carpenter, too.

Today, carpenters may work with many of these materials, or they may choose to specialize in one. For example, carpenters who build residential homes may be familiar with a wide variety of building materials, while carpenters who specialize as cabinetmakers primarily use only wood. Someone who works specifically with wood is called a woodworker. Carpenters use wood and other materials, such as brick, pressboard, and metal, to construct buildings, related structures, and the elements within them, such as stairways, cabinets, and doors. Whereas a woodworker might build a set of cabinets, it is a carpenter who will likely install them. Some carpenters also work on structures other than houses and buildings, including ships, highways, and bridges.

In carpentry, certain kinds of wood are used for specific jobs. For example, **hardwoods**, such as cherry, maple, and oak, are often used for flooring because they are strong and do not easily scratch. **Softwoods** include spruce, cedar, and pine. These are often used for outdoor projects, like building a deck, because they are able to endure the elements. A skilled carpenter chooses the right kind of wood or other material based on suitability and cost—hardwoods, for example, are typically more expensive than softwoods. The two names can often be deceiving because some hardwoods are softer than certain softwoods, and vice versa.

Today, environmental awareness and **sustainability** factor largely into the materials a carpenter uses, too. There is an increasing focus in the United States on conserving natural resources and developing sustainable and green building practices. Flooring is a good example of this. Years ago, houses were only built with wood floors. As the years went on, other building materials were used, such as carpet, linoleum, tile, and even

Bamboo is a more sustainable building material than many types of wood.

concrete. However, some people still want wood floors—in fact, they are highly sought after by many people purchasing homes—but wood, particularly certain varieties, is a disappearing natural resource. While we can replant forests, trees do not grow fast enough to meet the demand. Subsequently, other materials, such as bamboo, have been developed as an alternative to wood floors. Bamboo is sturdy and looks and feels very similar to wood, but it grows much more quickly and therefore is a much more sustainable material to use.

Using **reclaimed** wood, or wood that was recycled from another use, is also gaining in popularity—both because it's an environmentally friendly practice and because it adds certain style and history to a project. It's pretty cool to be able to say, "This coffee table was made from wood reclaimed from an 1800s New England schooner."

The environmental benefits are obvious: if you can use reclaimed wood in your project, that's one less tree that needs to be cut down. Yes, you're still using wood, but at least you're using wood that was already cut down. Otherwise, it may have ended up in the dump, recycled, or burned.

There's another benefit to using reclaimed wood: when you're working on a preservation project, you may need wood that is no longer available. Not all types of wood used in the past are still used today, so if you're trying to match a particular period's style, you may find that using reclaimed wood is the only way you can do so. For example, teak, mahogany, and sugar pine used to be readily available, but that is not the case now.

To build an average 2,000-square-foot (186-square-meter) house, about 13,000 **board feet** of lumber are needed. That works out to be about twenty-six 100-foot (30.5 meter) trees to build one house, which is a lot of

This staircase was built with reclaimed barnwood and steel.

wood. If you can replace some of that with reclaimed wood, the environment will thank you for it.

"Green" or sustainable builders keep considerations like this in mind: if a material isn't sustainable, what else can they use that is more environmentally friendly? As people in general become more environmentally conscious, the market for builders and contractors who use sustainable materials and practices will continue to grow.

Nowadays, there is also an increase in demand for a carpenter's skills, despite the fact that much of our furniture is mass-produced by machinery and even some of our houses are mass-constructed. And chances are, the need for carpenters will never go away—a skilled carpenter can never be completely replaced by a machine,

An Innovative Idea: Growing Furniture

In an effort to end wood waste, Gavin Munro, a furniture designer in the United Kingdom, opened a company called Full Grown and embarked on a creative new plan: "growing" furniture. Instead of harvesting trees, sending them through a mill, shaping the pieces, and assembling furniture, Munro manipulates trees to grow in the shapes needed for the furniture. He meticulously trims and prunes the trees so that they grow into the form he needs for the piece of furniture he's creating. The plus sides to this process are that it eliminates the wood wasted in the traditional furniture-making process, and it creates single-piece furniture that does not have any joints that can become loose over time. The downside is that Munro's customers must be patient—it takes from four to eight years to grow a piece of furniture, depending on the species of tree.

Full Grown offers tables, lamps, and mirror frames, and will soon offer chairs. Visit fullgrown.co.uk to see some of Munro's pieces and to learn more about this creative venture.

Gavin Munro "grows" furniture, such as these chairs.

no matter how far technology advances. A machine may be able to **prefabricate** cabinets or mass-produce the parts to construct a piece of furniture, but carpenters will always be needed to install those cabinets and to assemble the furniture out of the mass-produced parts.

Further, there is also a demand for carpenters from people who don't necessarily want their homes and everything in them to be created by a machine. Some people would rather spend the extra money for a custom-made piece of furniture handcrafted by a carpenter instead of purchasing a less expensive, mass-produced piece at a store like IKEA or Walmart. There is a growing specialty industry of **artisanal** carpenters and woodworkers who offer unique handcrafted products.

Another development that has changed the landscape of carpentry are permits and building codes. Permits are documents issued by a city's planning department that are often required before any construction, demolition, additions, or renovations are able to take place. Building codes are rules that have to be followed to ensure a project meets specific safety guidelines. Long ago, there were no such things as permits and building codes. If you had a plot of land and you wanted to build a house, you simply built a house. This is no longer the case. When you want to build a house today, you have to ensure that every aspect of that house meets local building codes, and you have to gather all of the required permits. These can be numerous, expensive, and difficult to obtain. For example, a family who purchased a plot of land in Bodega Bay, California, found out after they had purchased the land that it would cost $40,000 to obtain the necessary permits to put in a driveway. Yes, you read that right: $40,000! However, not all permits are that costly; Bodega Bay is a beach region that includes several protected wildlife areas, so it is a particularly difficult place to build. But in any area, you will need permits, and they are not free.

This is part of the reason why few people build their own houses anymore. The average person doesn't have an encyclopedic knowledge of building codes and permits, so the prospect of building a house seems daunting, if not impossible. A carpenter, on the other hand, knows about the codes and permits related to his or her part of the work and can help the homeowner navigate those tricky waters.

Tools, too, have changed the face of carpentry. Humans are thought to have used tools for about 3.4 million years, according to fossils recently discovered in Ethiopia. These fossils were bones discovered with deep scratch marks that historians believe were made by stone utensils. The first tools were simple and crudely formed. Tools have evolved (along with nearly everything else!) through the

TALKING WITH A CARPENTER: MIKE SWEENEY

Mike Sweeney has been a cabinetmaker, carpenter, and home remodeler at various stages of his life. He currently lives in the Santa Cruz Mountains of California. Here he offers some insight into what it's like to be a carpenter today.

What piqued your interest in carpentry and made you decide to pursue a career in it?

I didn't actually "pursue" a career in carpentry. When I have [worked as] a carpenter, it has been more a fallback position or a collision of circumstance and opportunity. However, I did pursue the skills that enabled me to fall back on it when I needed to. I needed a table once and decided to build it myself, so I bought some tools and read some how-to guides, and over a period of time, I acquired skills in using the new tools and learned some techniques. A friend was remodeling homes, and I worked with him, and over the years I developed more skills and techniques. Skill in anything is a cumulative process, and so it is with carpentry.

I spent my adolescent summers on a family farm in Illinois. On a farm, since there isn't always someone to call, you need to be able to do pretty much everything yourself. You need to be a carpenter, a mechanic, a rigger, a plumber, whatever the day calls for. My uncles and cousins had skills and tools, and I learned from them.

Carpentry is primarily building, repairing, or improving something and doing those things well—making a tight joint and using the right fasteners and materials generates a terrific satisfaction in me. I achieve pride and pleasure from having created something that didn't exist before, or from completing a repair or a project well and professionally.

Also, carpentry provides a sense of permanence and substance. Most of my career has been in the technology industry. I have been, over the years, well paid (much better paid than carpentry provides), but only a tiny fraction of the work I have done in technology still exists. However, the work I have done in carpentry and cabinetmaking still persists.

Did you specialize in a particular area?
In the late '80s and early '90s, I had a small cabinet shop in Livermore [California]. There, I built custom cabinets, furniture, and built-ins. I entered that area through need and opportunity. There was a recession in the tech field then, and I began building hardwood art boxes to sell. I had a friend who was a contractor, and he asked me to build a bar for a pool house he was building for a client. I did that, got some other projects, and set up shop. Again, the primary driver was satisfaction. Taking what was once a stack of raw lumber and hardwoods and in a few days putting the finishing touches on a new piece of furniture was enormously satisfying.

Talking with a Carpenter: Mike Sweeney

What did/do you like best about being a carpenter?

The satisfaction of building something substantial and permanent. Also, the process has its moments—figuring out methods or techniques for doing something tricky can also be rewarding. But mostly, it's the end result.

What don't you like about it? What's your least favorite part of the job?

Like good-news/bad-news jokes, what I like least about carpentry is part of what I like best about it: the process. Carpentry is hard work. It is very physical and involves lifting and moving heavy materials, working on ladders and scaffolds, holding heavy tools at awkward angles, even digging trenches and moving dirt. There is dust and noise and sweat, and it can be grueling. But that is the pathway to the completed project.

What changes (if any) have you seen in the field over the years you've been in it?

There have been a lot of changes in the materials used in carpentry over the years. When I was a kid on the farm, you had dimensioned wood of various types and a few sizes and types of plywood. Now there are manufactured wood products, particleboards, oriented strand board, flooring materials, deck materials, cement sidings—just a wide variety of specialized materials that result in higher quality with less effort. There is also a continual innovation in tools, fasteners, and adhesives.

But the essential and fundamental skills involved in carpentry haven't changed much. Pretty much everything you do starts with those fundamental skills, no matter which materials you're using. Without the fundamentals, no material or tool is going to get the job done right.

Any advice to people interested in possibly pursuing a career in carpentry?

Carpentry—or any of the trades, actually—requires a solid grounding in basic techniques, also known as skills. You have to be present and attentive, not only to perform the tasks well, but also because this trade can be dangerous. And there is no shortcut to developing the skills. I have found no other way than to learn by doing. You learn to drive nails by swinging a hammer and fastening two pieces of wood together. You learn to measure and cut by doing that. But mostly, you have to work with other seasoned carpenters and see how they do things. There is probably more information and technique transferred from one carpenter to another than is contained in all the books and magazines available.

years, but throughout most of history the main tools used by carpenters were simply hammers, nails, and saws. Nowadays, tools are complex and intricate. Take the evolution of the simple hammer. If you go into a well-stocked hardware store, you will find more than a dozen different types of hammers. The same is true of screwdrivers, drills, saws, wrenches, and pretty much any other tool you can think of.

And don't forget about power tools! Want a drill? Well, what kind? A manual hand drill, or a power drill with twenty-four different-sized bits? Is it a saw you need? OK, what type? A handsaw? A jigsaw? A band saw? Table saw? Miter saw? Once you sort out what they all do, power tools often help get a job done faster and with more accuracy than hand tools. However, some seasoned carpenters argue that the old ways are better, that carpentry done entirely by hand is far superior to the more mechanically produced pieces of today.

Carpenters today do more than use a level, a hammer, a saw, and some nails to build a project. They know which tool will work best for the job and how to use it. In many cases, that means power tools, but in some cases the traditional, manual style works best for the job. Carpenters learn these things from years of experience. They know the old way to build a box with a hammer, a saw, some nails, and a few pieces of wood, and they also know the newer ways to handle the same project using a compound miter saw to cut the angles so that corners meet tightly.

A lot may have changed in the world of carpentry over the years, but a couple of things haven't: it's still a tough, physical job, and the carpenter still experiences the pleasure of seeing an idea turned into a well-crafted, finished product.

Carpentry is a hands-on, manual job.

CHAPTER 2

Starting a Career in Carpentry

Starting a career in carpentry might sound fairly easy. You might think, "I like to build things, so I'll become a carpenter!" While building is a large part of the carpentry profession, the job isn't as simple as just picking up some tools and diving right in. You need to develop a skill set that will help you succeed in this field. The best way to do that is to look at your interests and then look for opportunities that can build on your strengths and help you develop the skills needed to become a carpenter.

Interests and Skills That Lend Themselves to a Career in Carpentry

If you like to work with your hands and see the end result of a project, carpentry could be the right career for you. This is not a desk job. While there may be some element of deskwork involved if you're working on design plans, in general, carpentry is an active, hands-on profession.

Because of the physical nature of carpentry, people interested in pursuing a career in the field should have good hand-eye coordination, excellent **visual-spatial** skills, good manual **dexterity**, and excellent physical fitness. Carpentry is a physically taxing profession. You're constantly using your muscles to haul and lift heavy materials, and to use tools. Swinging a hammer is easy the first few times; but after a few hundred swings, your arm will get a little tired!

There probably isn't a single carpenter on the planet who hasn't hammered his or her own thumb once or twice. Still, having good hand-eye coordination will help keep accidents to a minimum, and the same holds true for manual dexterity. If you are skilled with your hands, you will be less likely to make simple mistakes that can cause injuries.

Visual-spatial skills go hand in hand with manual dexterity and hand-eye coordination. Visual-spatial ability is what allows you to mentally manipulate objects in your mind. Think about Legos, which you may have played with as a child. When you sit down and lock together the Lego pieces, you're using manual dexterity. You're also using some level of hand-eye coordination, because your

Legos help children develop visual-spatial skills, hand-eye coordination, and manual dexterity—all necessary skills for a carpenter.

eyes see where to move your hands to make those pieces lock together, and your vision and hands work together to do so. Visual-spatial ability, on the other hand, is when you're thinking about what to do with those Legos. When you sat down in front of your bucket of Legos and thought, "I'm going to build a castle!" and envisioned that castle in your mind, you were using your visual-spatial ability to show you how to link those Legos together to create your castle. You weren't actually doing it yet, but you were picturing how to do it in your mind.

Carpenters need strong visual-spatial skills because they need to be able to see how the pieces of a project fit together. Think about a stairway or the frame of a roof. These are relatively complex parts of a house or building. The floor and walls are fairly straightforward, but the stairs and the roof require numerous pieces joined at different angles to create the finished product. Carpenters need to be able to visualize this to put it all together, as well as understand the techniques needed to do so correctly.

Additionally, it's helpful to be good at solving mathematical problems. Carpentry requires lots of measurements and calculations, so if math is something you struggle with, that may be a skill to work on if you're considering carpentry as a career. Knowing how to calculate angles is particularly important because most things you build will involve different angles and even curves. While in a perfectly easy world, everything would be built using simple 90-degree angles, that's just not reality. If it was, we'd all be living in square or rectangular boxes with little to no variation.

Attention to detail is also key for carpenters. There's a saying in the field: measure twice, cut once. This is because once a material is cut, it often cannot be reused if it was cut incorrectly. It's better to take the time and measure twice to make sure your measurements are accurate before you begin cutting. And particularly in certain areas of carpentry, an eye for detail is extremely important. Almost anyone can construct a simple bookshelf using two-by-fours and some nails, but it's the detail work that will make someone want to display that bookshelf in his or her home. It's not enough to simply know how to put a couple of boards together; you need to know how to create and work with the details that make a piece unique.

Problem-solving skills are also necessary as a carpenter. In the construction industry, deadlines must be met—on time and hopefully on budget. A skilled carpenter needs to be able to come up with fast solutions to any problems that arise.

Almost anyone can build a bookshelf, but a skilled carpenter can make a bookshelf a work of art.

AND NOW FOR SOMETHING A LITTLE DIFFERENT: TYLER FUQUA CREATIONS

Tyler FuQua lives and works outside of Portland, Oregon. He is both a carpenter and an artist—he creates custom woodworking projects as well as sets, giant puppets and props, costumes, and art installations for clients such as Nevada's annual weeklong Burning Man event, the Oregon Country Fair, and the band The String Cheese Incident. Here he offers details about his business.

This garden shed is one of Tyler FuQua's custom woodworking projects.

What do you enjoy about carpentry? What about the profession appeals to you?

There are a few reasons I enjoy being a carpenter. First off, I like creating things. I like taking raw materials and turning them into something useful, artful, or both. Second, I love wood.

I love the characteristics of the different species—the aroma of cedar, the density of an exotic hardwood, or the rich look of some reclaimed fir. I also love using tools. There is something to be said about using the right tool for the job. I often feel like Batman, but I have carpentry tools on my utility belt instead.

How do you come up with the ideas for your creations?
When it comes to the ideas for my creations, I often look to the natural world through an Alice in Wonderland filter. I like to use creatures that can be bigger than life. For instance, when I made The Racken (a giant octopus bike rack for Burning Man), I tried to think of an animal that would look as if it was coming out of the ground yet had enough body parts to hold a bunch of bikes. Sometimes I let my imagination go wild, as was the case with the twenty-foot-tall [6.1-meter-tall] Cosmic Space Frog. Part frog, part Godzilla, that creature was definitely not from this planet.

What sorts of materials do you like to use for your creations?
I love to use reclaimed materials whenever possible. My best use of these was for my alien insect costume, Thorax. Built entirely out of reclaimed materials, Thorax had strainers for eyes, pizza screens on his legs, and the back mat of a Subaru, to name a few things. I like when people can see what I did with an ordinary object to make it something very unordinary. I have recently invested in the ability to weld aluminum, which is strong and lightweight. I started off using anything I had

And Now for Something a Little Different: Tyler FuQua Creations

around the house—wood, PVC pipe, wire—and then graduated to weldable steel. But steel is really heavy. So that is where aluminum comes into play. Next up: carbon fiber!

Do you have a favorite creation you've made?

I love all of my creations and recently had to say goodbye to some early ones due to lack of space, which was sad. But I think one of my favorites was made last year. His name is Grunt the Recycle-a-Bull, and he is a costume puppet. He has a large bull's

Grunt the Recycle-a-Bull is made out of recycled materials and is one of FuQua's most complex creations.

head and a giant shell made from recyclables. His eyelids and mouth are controlled by bike cables that are in my hand. This allows him to speak and show emotion. This was my most complex creation as far as detailed expression goes.

Thorax, FuQua's alien insect costume, is also made out of reclaimed materials.

Any advice to students who are interested in possibly pursuing a career in carpentry?

Advice on becoming a carpenter? How about this: become a plumber! They make a lot of money! Just kidding. A good carpenter is patient. Measure twice, cut once, for the board stretcher hasn't been invented yet. (I'm working on it!) And use the right tool for the job. It will make the job easier, and the piece will look better in the end. Try to find a good carpenter to apprentice under. Sure, you can learn by trial and error, but you might as well learn from someone who has already made all of those mistakes.

If you think you might be interested in a career as a carpenter, try out some basic building projects and see whether you enjoy them. You can easily search online for step-by-step instructions for simple projects, such as a doghouse or shed. These projects are generally straightforward and don't require too many materials, so you can play around with them without spending a lot of money.

Education

If you're interested in a career in a hands-on job like carpentry, you probably aren't going to follow the trajectory of getting your high school degree and entering a four-year university program to earn a bachelor's degree. There are a couple of educational paths you can take to work your way toward a carpentry career.

Secondary Education

While you're still in middle school and high school, there may be classes available to take that will help you learn some of the fundamental basics of carpentry. If your school offers a woodshop class, for example, that would be a great place to start. Unfortunately, though, woodshop classes are disappearing from American schools. In some areas, applied skills, such as woodworking and metalworking, are not as valued as theoretical subjects in high schools. In California, for example, high schools focus their efforts on administering classes that meet the University of California and California State University systems "a-g requirements," which focus on academic subjects and performing arts, rather than shop classes.

California is not the only state where this is an issue, though. Across the country, school districts are focusing on college prep and eliminating vocational and shop classes so that budgets for other classes can be reallocated to other areas. But if you're one of the lucky few whose high school still offers shop classes, then sign up for woodshop and/or metal shop to learn some of the foundational skills and get some hands-on building practice.

The great thing about a woodshop or metal shop class is that you'll usually have some flexibility in what you want to build. Your teacher will likely have some basic guidelines for the types of projects you need to complete, but often you can get creative and customize your projects. Also, many shop teachers will let you come in at lunch or after school and use the tools to do extra projects if you so desire.

If your school doesn't offer shop classes, look around in your community and see if you can find some woodworking classes. Your local parks and recreation

If your school doesn't offer shop classes, do some research and see if your community offers classes through its parks and recreation department or adult education courses.

department may offer them, and many regions also allow teenagers to enroll in adult education courses if space permits. It's worth a try.

You might be surprised to learn that algebra, geometry, business math, physics, and technology classes can also help you prepare for a career in this field. In a very simplified view, carpentry involves working with shapes and numbers. You use shapes to build things, and you use numbers to calculate lengths, angles, and so on. So you can see how classes like geometry and math would be helpful! Physics, too, is useful because you need to understand how an object will react when placed in a certain position. For example, physics tells us that we cannot place a large square object on the tip of a triangle; the square will tip, and its force will cause the structure to collapse. This is useful knowledge for budding carpenters!

Technology classes can be helpful, too, because construction jobs can involve designing **blueprints** or working from them. Being familiar with computer-aided drafting and design (**CADD**) software can help with these tasks, and if you're lucky, your school may offer some basic courses in CADD. If not, such courses are readily available at many community colleges and technical schools.

If you can't find a CADD class, see if you can find some CADD software to play around with. Many types of computer software are surprisingly self-explanatory, or you can find great tutorials on the web. You may be able to learn a lot through self-teaching, at least enough to give you a foundation until you can find a good CADD class.

In short, your math and technology classes are all going to help you if you're looking at a career in carpentry. English classes are always helpful, too. You need to be able to put together a good résumé, for example. But math and technology classes will be the most immediately applicable to the field you're considering.

Physical education courses are also useful if you're interested in a career in carpentry. Because of the hands-on, physical nature of this career, you need to be in good shape to be a successful carpenter, and you need a great deal of stamina and strength. The quickest way to get a back injury on the job is to be out of shape. Keeping yourself in good condition is crucial in this type of physically demanding profession.

Be sure not to discount summer school and technical programs, either! There are summer programs where middle-school and high-school students can learn carpentry skills in a community-service setting. For example, the VISIONS Service Adventures program combines community service with travel and cultural immersion. Participating students travel to under-resourced communities in the United States, as well as abroad, to live and work in a host community.

Post-Secondary Education

After high school, it is often difficult to land an apprenticeship with an experienced carpenter. While becoming a carpenter doesn't require a university degree, it does help to have some sort of post-secondary education in the field. Many aspiring carpenters choose to go to trade schools that offer certificate programs. Most of these schools require a high-school diploma or GED as a prerequisite for entry, and the programs generally take about one year to complete.

The certificate programs are very hands-on, and students usually learn about framing, laying out walls and rafters, and estimating the cost of materials. Some schools offer specialized certificate programs for skills such as framing, or interior or exterior finishing. In general, the courses taught in a certificate program include classes about tools, construction materials, carpentry techniques, reading blueprints, and performing calculations. Some programs offer CADD training, and some offer courses on applicable laws and business codes related to carpentry.

Through a certificate program, students can earn apprenticeships with construction firms or master carpenters, or they may choose to work as handymen or carpentry assistants.

For students who prefer a degree in the field, some schools offer associate degrees in carpentry. These programs cover many of the same topics that are covered in certificate programs, but they may offer further education opportunities, too, such as classes in management, project scheduling, and cost estimation. Students in associate degree programs also take general education classes, which are not typically required in certificate programs.

For example, Columbus Technical College in Georgia offers a two-year carpentry diploma program.

Students take courses in foundations of math, English, and computers; safety; professional tool use; materials and fasteners; professional development; floor and wall framing; footings and foundations; site layout; ceiling and roof framing; interior finishes; exterior finishes and trims; stairs; concrete forming; rigging and reinforcing; and doors and door hardware.

An associate degree in carpentry can be useful if you hope to someday work as a manager. Many management positions require you to have some sort of a degree, so if that's the path you're interested in, earning an associate degree may make a lot of sense for you.

Students in associate programs can sometimes skip the apprenticeship phase and head straight into a job in the field. However, some students still complete an apprenticeship, either because it's required for a particular job or because they want to gain more experience and make their skills more marketable. The value of the hands-on training and experience you can gain through an apprenticeship cannot be emphasized enough.

Online Learning

There are no carpentry certificate programs available online. The hands-on training offered in these programs simply cannot be offered electronically. There are, however, carpentry diploma programs offered online, such as from Penn Foster Career School. This diploma program can be combined with apprenticeships and/or on-the-job training to give aspiring carpenters the education and hands-on training they need to work in the industry.

Generally, online carpentry diploma programs teach students about building codes, layouts, materials, and how to construct objects. They also require students to complete hands-on, practical exercises on their own, using specified materials. So there is a hands-on component to the program; it's just not done in person, under the one-on-one guidance available from an instructor in a traditional program.

Deciding on the Best Program

There is no single answer to the question "what is the best program for an aspiring carpenter?" As in any career, a lot depends on the individual person's circumstances and interests. However, there are some questions to keep in mind as you decide what sort of carpentry program you might want to pursue:

- Is the school **accredited**? In general, no matter what field you're considering for your future, it's best to go with an accredited school.

- Does the school provide financial assistance? You may or may not need this, but it's certainly an important question to ask if you do!
- How long is the school's program?
- How is the school's reputation in the industry? Do its alumni have a good track record of finding employment upon completion of the program?
- Does the school help students secure apprenticeships? What about employment upon finishing the program?
- Is the school affiliated with a local labor **union**?
- Does the school provide training materials and tools, or are students responsible for purchasing them separately?
- What are the school's facilities like? Are you expected to complete projects on-site? If so, is the work area well equipped and usable?

Apprenticeships

Students interested in a carpentry career often begin an apprenticeship, either straight out of high school, after earning a certificate from a trade school, or after obtaining their associate degree in carpentry. Apprenticeships allow budding carpenters to work (for pay!) for several years alongside experienced or master carpenters, furthering the apprentice's skills. Many apprenticeships include some amount of classroom

Finding a good apprenticeship can be an invaluable step in building your career in carpentry.

instruction in topics related to the field of carpentry, but some apprenticeships are strictly hands-on opportunities to work alongside experienced professionals.

Apprenticeship programs are usually offered through either construction unions or commercial or industrial building contractor firms. It may take some hunting to find an apprenticeship—they can be few and far between. You can expect an apprenticeship to last four or five years.

If you are lucky enough to land an apprenticeship, upon completing that apprenticeship you may be able to gain employment as a **journeyman**. A journeyman carpenter is simply a classification for a carpenter who has completed an apprenticeship program. Journeymen work in any of the environments that experienced carpenters work in, such as office buildings, homes, tunnels, and mills.

Certification and Licensing

According to the US Bureau of Labor Statistics (BLS), certification isn't required for carpenters. However, there are certifications available, and many carpenters choose to pursue them. Some certifications include those for specialized fields of carpentry, such as scaffolding, and those for green and sustainable building, such as the US Green Building Council's Leadership in Energy and Environmental Design (LEED) certification. Also, the National Center for Construction Education and Research offers credentials to carpenters when they complete a four-level curriculum covering content about building materials, cabinet fabrication, and advanced wall systems. The National Association of the Remodeling Industry offers, among other certifications, a Certified Lead Carpenter (CLC) certification that requires a combination of experience, completion of a comprehensive application, and successful completion of a half-day examination. There are further certifications available in

Occupational Safety and Health Administration (OSHA) and Hazardous Communication (HCS or HAZCOM).

Licensing isn't required for carpenters in all states, although most do have some sort of licensing requirement. For many states, a carpenter needs to have a contractor license. Even if in general the state doesn't require a license, certain tasks, such as demolition and some types of renovation, require carpenters to be licensed. Carpenters must also be licensed if they are working as general contractors. In general, though, it's a good idea to get licensed, even if it's not required in your particular state. People are much more likely to hire a licensed carpenter than an unlicensed one. Finding out that you're licensed will give potential clients some peace of mind—if you're licensed, they assume you must know what you're doing!

Trade Organizations and Unions

Many industries, including carpentry, have trade organizations and unions. These are two different things, although sometimes they overlap in certain functions.

Unions act as a collective force in an industry and work to support fair labor practices and wages, job safety, and job security. Union members also receive on-the-job training through apprenticeships, which are generally more comprehensive than the apprenticeships offered by other companies or organizations.

Many carpenters are members of the United Brotherhood of Carpenters and Joiners of America (UBC), which boasts about half a million members in the construction industry in North America. The UBC was established in the late 1800s to support woodworkers, homebuilders, and carpenters. Other carpenters' unions include the Associated General Contractors of America (AGC) and the National Association of Home Builders (NAHB).

If you choose to work in the carpentry field, you can choose to join your local chapter of the UBC. Membership in a union is never required, but often people working in a particular unionized industry find it beneficial to join. As a member, you are required to pay union dues, but in return the union can act as your voice in any labor and/or salary disputes, and you'll be eligible for job-training opportunities as well.

One difficult aspect of joining a union occurs when members call for a strike. You may have heard the phrase "cross the picket line." This comes from unions, where sometimes members have to strike and participate in picket lines to fight for fair wages and work conditions that they believe they are entitled to. If you choose to cross a picket line and go to work when the rest of the union is striking, you might find yourself on the receiving end of some very cold shoulders.

Trade organizations, on the other hand, are founded and funded by the businesses in a particular industry. Therefore, a carpentry trade organization is funded by carpenters. A trade organization, also sometimes called a trade association, may offer conferences or classes to its members, and will usually promote networking between its members. Trade organizations also often handle advertising and publishing for its members. Much like unions require union dues, trade organizations usually charge membership fees. In the carpentry field, trade organizations include the Institute of Carpenters and numerous regional organizations.

As in any industry, networking can be incredibly valuable. It may be worth joining a trade organization for the connections you can make. You never know where your next job might come from!

A carpenter works in all types of environments, both indoors and outdoors.

CHAPTER 3

On the Job

One of the great things about a career in carpentry is that no two days are exactly alike. Even if you specialize in a particular field of carpentry, such as cabinetmaking, you're not going to spend every day building the exact same kind of cabinets. There will be variety in your job. If you're a master carpenter, there can even be quite a bit of variety in your job, since you're then experienced enough to pick and choose the projects you most enjoy working on.

When searching for your ideal career, another aspect to consider is whether you want a job that keeps you inside or outside. If you find office spaces confining and dislike the idea of sitting behind a desk all day, then evidently a desk job is not for you. If you're a carpenter, you are likely

What Is a Master Carpenter?

A master carpenter is, simply put, a professional with a wealth of experience in the field of carpentry. In general, carpenters begin their career as apprentices then work their way up to become journeymen. After working as journeymen for many years, usually somewhere between four and ten years, and attaining a high level of skill, journeymen can be considered master carpenters. To do so, they must be a licensed contractor in their region and a member of the union.

In the United States, there is no specific exam or certification required to be considered a master carpenter; the requirements vary by region. In general, a journeyman who is approaching master carpenter status will apply to the carpenter's union and will need to show that he or she has taught apprentices, completed jobs valued over a certain dollar amount, and achieved various accolades in his or her career.

Put simply, a master carpenter is a master of the trade.

very rarely sitting behind a desk. Or if you *are* sitting behind one, it's because you're *building* it!

Perhaps the biggest plus in carpentry is that every day you get to see something in your mind become a reality as you work to build a particular item or structure.

When you are finished with a project, you have an end product that you can touch, be it a house, a set of cabinets, a piece of furniture, a ship, or pretty much anything you can dream up.

A Day in the Life

Because many carpenters specialize in different areas, it's difficult to describe a typical day in the life. A framer would have a very different workday from a cabinetmaker. Let's look at what may be involved in a day in the life of a master carpenter working on a remodel in a residential kitchen.

You will likely start your day bright and early, as most construction jobs require that you arrive on-site early. Construction work can be *hot* in the spring and summer, which are typically busy building periods in areas where winters are particularly cold or receive a lot of snow. Working earlier in the day allows workers to avoid the afternoon heat. It's important to eat a hearty breakfast; carpentry is a very physical profession, and you'll need energy on the job.

You will need to be on the jobsite; as the master carpenter, you're responsible for supervising the other carpenters and the apprentices who are working on the project. To start, you might have to review blueprints for

Carpenters must sometimes review blueprints for a project.

the kitchen to ensure the plans meet local building codes. If everything is not to code, the building inspector will not sign off on the project.

Once you make the adjustments to the design in order to meet building codes, you have to run it past the architect and other higher-ups on the team. Luckily, you don't have to deal directly with the client—someone else takes care of that. This is just fine with you, since you like building and working with your coworkers, but dealing directly with clients isn't high on your list of favorite things to do.

After a quick lunch break to refuel, you may have some manual work to do. The foundation for the house was poured some time ago, and the exterior walls have been framed out, but you're now ready to start framing in the kitchen. While you work on the framing, the other carpenters on your team can begin working on other components of the job, such as building the door frames or building custom cabinets that will be installed later.

This kind of project isn't accomplished in a single afternoon. It will be completed over the coming days (or weeks, depending on the project). It's hard, satisfying work, and you enjoy seeing the design take physical shape, but you also have to deal with constant questions from the apprentice working under you. For an apprentice, putting his or her book skills to work in a real on-the-job environment includes a learning curve and a lot of oversight from you as his or her teacher.

By the time you finish for the day, you're likely physically and mentally exhausted. You're physically tired from a day of sawing, nailing, drilling, and working with heavy lumber, and you're mentally spent from overseeing your apprentice and from working out the calculations addressing the minor tweaks needed to bring the kitchen up to code. Despite being tired, you can take pride in a job well done.

A cabinetmaker builds and installs cabinets.

You will sleep well that night, after a long day of hard work … until the alarm rings early tomorrow, to start all over again.

Carpentry Specializations

The field of carpentry is wide open with a variety of specializations available. These specializations, some of which are quite focused, include:

Cabinetmaker: Cabinetmakers build wooden cabinets, as well as fine furniture. Some cabinetmakers further specialize in certain areas, such as the restoration or reproduction of antique furniture.

It Won't Always Be a Man's World

If you're a woman and interested in getting into the carpentry field, you're among a select few. Carpentry is traditionally a male-dominated field. The 2000 US Census showed that only 1.5 percent of people who identified themselves as working in the carpentry field were females. That number has actually shrunk slightly in the past decade, too—as of 2011, female carpenters made up only 1.4 percent of the field, according to the BLS.

The women who *are* in carpentry sometimes face discrimination, harassment, and limited career advancement. Because women have not been traditionally taught carpentry skills, there's a common stereotype that women don't make capable carpenters. However, some women are working in the field to change that perception and bring new women into the profession.

It might seem intimidating to be a woman working in a traditionally male-dominated field. If you own your own business (or are at least a majority stakeholder in the company), you can be certified as a **WBE** (Woman's Business Enterprise), which can be beneficial when it comes to bidding jobs. When clients put out **RFPs** (Requests for Proposals), they often will give some preference to WBE or **MBE** (Minority Business Enterprise) firms.

Cooper: Coopers make and repair casks (such as for wine) and barrels.

Finish carpenter/trim carpenter: Finish carpenters and trim carpenters work specifically on a structure's finishes, such as trim, molding, baseboards, mantels, shelves, and paneling.

Formwork carpenter: Formwork carpenters build the frames that hold wet concrete for building foundations. They must ensure that the frames are adequately reinforced with iron and steel so that the structure's foundation is solid.

Coopers make barrels and casks, which are often used to age wine and spirits.

Framers build the "skeleton" of a house.

Framer: A framer, or framing carpenter, builds or repairs the frame of a structure. When you see the "skeleton" of a newly constructed house, you're seeing the framer's work on display.

Green carpenter: A green carpenter does the same type of work as any carpenter, but he or she specializes in using environmentally friendly and sustainable building materials. In today's environmentally conscious world, green carpenters are more in demand than ever.

Joiner: Joiners make wooden parts of a structure, such as stairs, window frames, and doorframes. Carpenters then take these components and install them in the structure. Essentially, the joiner makes the pieces that the carpenter puts together at the jobsite.

The field of carpentry is strongly dominated by men, but there are female carpenters, such as Maria Klemperer-Johnson, actively and successfully working in the field. She started her career building cabinets in New York, learning cabinet building and joinery. She took classes in timber framing at Heartwood School for the Homebuilding Crafts in Massachusetts, where she was generally the only female student. She eventually moved on to working in home construction and founded the Double Dog Timberworks contracting company.

In 2013, Klemperer-Johnson began offering carpentry classes for women through Double Dog. The first class had eight women enrolled, and they used a 1987 camper-trailer

Maria Klemperer-Johnson teaches students to build tiny houses, so they can learn and practice their carpentry skills on a small scale.

as the base to build a 165-square-foot (15.3 sq m) tiny house. The students in that inaugural class came from all different backgrounds and reported that they felt very comfortable learning in the all-female environment.

Klemperer-Johnson uses the tiny-house model to teach because tiny houses use few resources, can be built any time during the year, and allow students to learn a wide range of skills on a small scale. She hopes to continue offering the classes and eventually have students in them become paid apprentices at Double Dog.

Klemperer-Johnson's program, which is now called the Hammerstone School, is not the only one for women interested in carpentry. The Heartwood School, Yestermorrow Design/Build School in Vermont, and the Workshop for Women in Colorado all offer carpentry classes specifically for women. In New York City, a branch of Nontraditional Employment for Women (NEW) also offers a free, six-week pre-apprentice program for women who want to pursue a career in the carpentry field.

In 2012, the United States Department of Labor announced $1.8 million in grants for women who wish to pursue nontraditional careers. The grant money was divided between six organizations that help support women pursuing careers in the nontraditional fields of manufacturing, transportation, and construction.

The reality for women interested in pursuing a career in carpentry is changing, although slowly. Men still dominate the field at this time, but women are slowly starting to make their mark in the industry.

Luthiers build stringed instruments, such as guitars, which usually include a neck and hollow sound box.

Log builder: Log builders build cabins, barns, and other structures out of stacked logs.

Luthier: A luthier crafts stringed instruments, such as guitars, violins, and cellos, out of wood. Luthiers also repair such instruments.

Preservation/restoration carpenter: Preservation carpenters specialize in building, restoring, and preserving historic structures. These carpenters are skilled at replicating and matching the finishes on structures to preserve their **historic integrity**.

Scenic carpenter: Scenic carpenters build sets for plays, movies, and television shows. Being a scenic carpenter can allow you to tap into your creative side more than some of the other specializations can. Scenic carpenters are used on most movie, television, and theater sets, and particularly on whimsical or fantastical productions such as the *Star Wars* films, *Alice in Wonderland*, or the *Harry Potter* films.

Shipwright/ship's carpenter: Shipwrights or ship's carpenters build and repair ships and components of ships. Some assemble ships on dry land and some work on running ships, making emergency repairs or building additional parts as necessary.

Shipwrights build wooden boats or ships of all shapes and sizes.

PAUL SELLERS: PASSION FOR WOODWORKING

Paul Sellers describes himself as a "lifelong amateur woodworker," but he's much more than that. He's an accomplished blogger and the author of the 2011 book *Working Wood*. His instructional videos on woodworking have attracted thousands of viewers—at recent count, his YouTube channel had nearly 94,000 subscribers. He's also a woodworking instructor who has taught students in the United States, Canada, and Europe. He started the New Legacy School of Woodworking at his workshop in Penrhyn Castle in North Wales. On top of all that, Sellers also designed and built pieces for the Cabinet Room at the White House!

Sellers doesn't only make cabinets, though. He has also crafted canoes and even built a cello for his son. So he's a cabinetmaker, shipwright, and luthier—just to name a few specializations!

To watch Sellers' videos or follow his woodworking blog, visit his website at paulsellers.com. You won't be disappointed!

Job Hazards

As with any profession, carpenters face occupational hazards as part of their day-to-day work. Some of the hazards are obvious, such as the use of machinery with sharp blades or points, but others are less so. For instance, carpenters might be exposed to loud noise from power tools; use or work close to substances that could cause injuries or health problems, such as solvents or lead-based paint; and work in awkward or potentially unsafe positions. That said, the risk posed by many of these hazards can be minimized by adopting preventative measures and observing good work practices.

Safety First

Wearing protective gear and following safety procedures are essential on the job. Carpenters should always wear protective eyewear, such as safety goggles, when working. If you are operating power tools or working in a loud environment, protect your hearing by wearing earplugs or earmuffs. Steel-toed footwear is also usually required in most construction zones. One of the simplest ways to avoid accidents is by using your common sense. Keep your work area clean and clutter-free and make sure all tools and their parts are in good working order. Do not wear loose clothing that might get caught in a machine.

Safety first is a requirement in carpentry and any other construction-related career.

Also, ensure you know how to properly use equipment. For example, if a carpenter is working with a chainsaw, he or she must be aware of the danger of the saw "kicking back." Kicking back occurs when the blade of the saw becomes pinched by the wood or other material it is cutting. This causes the saw to pull away, or kick back, from the material toward the operator. This can result in serious, and sometimes fatal, injuries. Fortunately, many tools now include additional safety features, such as automatic shutoffs, to prevent workplace injuries.

With any career you choose, there will be benefits and drawbacks. It's important to evaluate what's most important to *you* before you make a decision on the right career for you.

A growing population increases the need for new homes.

CHAPTER 4

Carpentry Now and in the Future

When you consider embarking on any career, it's important to look at the future prospects for that profession. You don't want to spend your time and energy preparing for a career that's not likely to yield a strong, positive future for you. Of course, your main consideration should be whether a career will make you happy—you have a lot of working years ahead of you, and you might as well do something you enjoy.

However, happiness isn't the only factor to consider. Compensation is important, too. Money can't buy happiness, as the saying goes, but it certainly helps. You don't want to choose a career that will leave you scrambling to make ends meet every month; you want a career that will pay you enough to live comfortably.

In addition to compensation, you should also consider the growth potential of the career you are considering. Some jobs are considered dying industries, such as travel agents and newspaper publishing. That's not to say you *can't* find work in those industries, but the numbers of jobs in them are shrinking. To set yourself up for success, try to choose a field that has a steady growth potential.

Projected Employment Growth for Carpenters

If you're interested in becoming a carpenter, here's some good news: the BLS's *Occupational Outlook Handbook* predicts a 24 percent growth in carpentry jobs between 2012 and 2022. That's more than double the predicted 11 percent growth for all occupations in the United States!

Part of the reason for this impressive job growth is the need for new-home construction to accommodate the ever-growing population. Although people in the United States have fewer children than people in many other countries, which leads to slower population growth, the immigration rate in the United States is quite high. Therefore, the overall growth rate of the United States population is steadily increasing—and those people naturally need places to live.

Also, people living in older homes are likely to hire carpenters to help them renovate or remodel their homes. There was an enormous baby boom after World War II, and that population growth continued into the 1950s and 1960s. Many homes were built in the following decades to accommodate the growing population. Today, many of these homes are outdated and in need of updating and repair.

Around the middle of the twentieth century, there was also enormous growth in **infrastructure**, such as roads and bridges, and many of those roads and bridges are now

Growth in building also means growth in infrastructure.

in need of upgrades and repairs, which requires the work of skilled carpenters. And with **urban sprawl** pushing the outer limits of cities farther and farther out, there are certainly new roads and bridges being planned and built.

There is one factor that slightly slows the growth in the field, though: the use of prefabricated building materials, such as cabinets and stairs. Carpenters used to build these on-site when working on a home or structure, but today they are often manufactured in a factory off-site and simply installed by a carpenter or contractor.

Also, job growth in the field of carpentry is affected by region. More populated areas typically require more building and thus more carpenters. Less densely populated regions may not have as much job potential for carpenters. So you're more likely to find work in, say, the New York or Chicago areas than you are out in the middle of rural Wyoming.

Despite these challenges, overall the projected growth in the field of carpentry is positive and shows no signs of slowing down.

Earnings

As wages go, carpenters' earnings are about average. The **median** annual wage for carpenters in 2012 was just under $40,000. That's about $5,000 per year more than

Female carpenters aren't only on the rise in the United States. In Egypt, a half-Egyptian, half-Italian woman named Maha Shoukry is making a name for herself by being the *only* well-known female carpenter in that country. For her company, ByPapousa, Shoukry creates pieces of furniture that combine traditional elements with contemporary design.

Shoukry, who was raised in Pakistan, Switzerland, and Italy, married an American and lived in Singapore, the Philippines, and Spain, where she took art courses including carpentry. She moved to Egypt in 1999 and got her start by designing pieces for friends. Then she moved on to working for large commercial properties. Egypt is well known for furniture factories, but Shoukry's work is in high demand by **expats**, newlyweds, and families with children.

Despite people's appreciation for her work, Shoukry's gender has been a challenge in getting her business going. In Egypt, where gender roles are more divided than they are in the United States, wood merchants would quote her very high prices for raw materials, simply because she was a woman. Shoukry solved the problem by hiring a male factory manager to procure her raw materials.

In a perfect world, Shoukry's work would stand on its own merits, and the fact that she is a woman wouldn't be an issue. However, the world is not perfect, and some changes take longer to make than others. Shoukry has found a solution that works for her and continues to build her business steadily, opening doors for future female **entrepreneurs** in Egypt, and in the meantime creating unique, inspired furniture.

Skilled carpenters earn wages slightly above the national average. As you acquire more skills, your pay will likely increase.

the median annual wage for all occupations in the United States. Apprentices typically make 50 to 70 percent less than experienced carpenters, but their pay increases as their skills do. There are certainly industries where interns are paid nothing as they gain experience, so the fact that carpentry apprentices earn a salary is a bonus. Also, you may start working at a very low rate, but there's definitely room for growth as you learn more about the field.

Another factor to consider is that overtime is common in carpentry if you're working to meet construction deadlines. Depending on how you're employed as a carpenter, you may receive overtime pay (which can be 1.5 to 2 times your basic hourly rate).

If you're interested in a more specialized field of carpentry, the salary may vary. For example, cabinetmakers are considered woodworkers for the purposes of the BLS, and their median pay in 2012 was just over $28,000 per year—lower than the average salary across all occupations. The BLS breaks down hourly wages for woodworkers into the following categories and amounts:

- Cabinetmakers and bench carpenters: $14.90
- Furniture finishers: $13.70
- Woodworking machine setters, operators, and tenders (except sawing): $13.00
- Sawing machine setters, operators, and tenders: $12.59

As is true for many jobs, the pay for carpenters depends on the region in which you live and the sector in which you work. Carpenters in certain major metropolitan areas tend to earn higher salaries. According to *U.S. News & World Report* magazine, these areas include Honolulu, Hawaii; Anchorage, Alaska; and New York City, New York. In fact, in 2012, the New York City District Council of Carpenters signed a five-year contract with a major employer that raised compensation for its twenty-five thousand members to $99.16 per hour, which equates to more than $200,000 in annual salary.

Additionally, carpenters who work in the film and video industry, primarily in the Los Angeles area, enjoy

An area's cost of living is important to take into account when projecting what you can earn as a carpenter.

wages that are approximately $26,000 more than the national average for carpenters.

However, keep in mind that some of these major metropolitan areas are also expensive to live in. You might earn more money as a carpenter in Honolulu, New York City, or Hollywood, but you'll also spend more to live there than you would in a more rural location. Your higher wages could be significantly offset by the increased cost of living in a particular area.

Something New: 3-D Printed Wood

You may have heard of **3-D printing**, where a solid object is created from a digital file by a printer laying down many layers of material as it creates the object. This relatively new technology is also being applied in the field of carpentry. A Belgian 3-D technology company recently released a test product of 3-D printed wood models created from a very fine powder made from wood chips. The material looks a bit like sand, but it is actually a wood product. The company is still experimenting with the product, but currently it is being used to develop complex wood models that are difficult or impossible to create using traditional woodworking methods.

Employment Options

When it comes to working as a carpenter, you have two main options: you can work for someone else or you can work for yourself. Both options have their pros and cons, so the type of employment you wish to have is not a decision to be taken lightly.

In 2012, about 36 percent of carpenters were self-employed, and the rest were traditionally employed.

Tara Betterman: Female in the Field

Tara Betterman is the founder of Betterman Builders in Indianapolis, Indiana. As a child, she learned painting, plumbing, electrical, and carpentry skills by following her father around as he worked as a maintenance technician for a property-management group. Tara founded Communitas Management Inc., a property-management company, in 2003 and followed up with Betterman Builders, its maintenance, repair, and remodeling sister organization. Betterman Builders does everything from roofing, drywall, and painting, to remodeling, carpentry, and general contracting. As Tara says, "If you can think it, we can build it."

Do you work in multiple areas of carpentry, or do you specialize in one particular area?

I prefer finish carpentry. Most carpenters can do all kinds but prefer one specific kind. We have great framing carpenters on staff.

Have you always wanted to be a carpenter? What inspired you to want to become one?

I'm not really a carpenter by trade. I'm a general contractor, so I know a lot about most of the trades. Most of my personal carpentry work is done for the benefit of friends and family.

What is your favorite part of your carpentry work?

My favorite part is the planning and design of a project. A good carpenter is analytical and detail-oriented.

Any downsides? Anything you really *don't* like doing?

I don't like putting band-aids on things. What I mean by that is that if it's not right, I'll rip it apart and start over again.

Carpentry has traditionally been a very male-dominated field. What are your thoughts on that? Have you experienced any difficulty being a woman in a male-dominated field? Do you see any positive change happening in this regard?

In the beginning, I did see a lot of discrimination when I started in the '90s. I think you have to prove yourself—prove that you can do the work. In the end, I've found that most people appreciate working with a female tradesperson because of my attention to detail and aesthetics.

Any words of advice for aspiring carpenters?

Become well-rounded. Do framing, custom work, inside work, outside work, cabinets. The more well-rounded you are, the bigger asset you'll be to a company. Versatility will make you able to command a better salary.

If you're self-employed, you will *not* receive overtime pay, and you'll have to pay higher taxes because you'll be liable for roughly 15 percent in self-employment tax over and above your regular federal and state taxes. You might also have to purchase your own health insurance.

If you're traditionally employed, you may be eligible for overtime pay (depending on how your job is classified), and you will *not* have to pay self-employment tax. You may or may not have to provide your own health insurance—many employers still offer some sort of insurance coverage to employees for a fee. Your pay will likely be steady, and employers typically offer other benefits such as paid time off and perhaps contributions to retirement funds. Finally, depending on how the company is set up, you will likely not be responsible for "growing the business," as you would be if self-employed. If selling yourself isn't your strong point, this is certainly something to consider. Self-employed people not only have to do the work, they have the added responsibility of bringing in clients, which requires a lot of people skills and networking.

Self-employment includes several perks as well. You might enjoy more flexibility and potentially earn higher pay. If you're a self-employed carpenter, you have more opportunity to set the days and hours you work, and possibly even to choose which jobs and clients you want to work with. You don't answer to an employer—you answer only to yourself (with consideration for your clients, of course!). You may also be paid more, even if it might not be at a steady rate (so you might need to become adept at financial planning and budgeting). Traditionally, contract employees receive slightly higher pay rates than regular employees because the employer doesn't have to pay for the contract employee's health benefits, Social Security tax, and so on.

So there's a tradeoff. Being employed by someone else may keep you steadily employed, but you'll have to work

Carpenters can be traditionally employed or can start their own businesses and be their own bosses.

the hours you're assigned, and you may get a lower pay rate. However, you'll save on taxes and potentially on health insurance, and you'll possibly receive other side benefits, so it may work out to be more beneficial to you in the long run. You simply need to assess your personal situation and the employment opportunities available and decide what best fits you.

Job Search Tips

Naturally, an apprenticeship will be extremely beneficial to your future career in carpentry. If you're lucky, perhaps your apprenticeship will lead to a job offer for you. But what if you're not that lucky? What if your apprenticeship was a good experience, but it didn't lead to a job offer? Well, then you're stuck doing what most people do: embarking on the almighty job hunt.

Creating a Résumé

When it comes time to apply for jobs, you'll need a résumé. You may need one earlier than that, when you're working on getting an apprenticeship, but if you don't have one by the time you start job hunting, then now's the time.

Dozens of books have been written on how to craft a good résumé; for a detailed description of how to do so, check one out. For now, here are the highlights.

A good résumé will concisely and clearly show a potential employer who you are and why they should hire you. But how do you do that? How do you sum up everything important about who you are and why you're a good candidate for a job in just a page or two? Simple: you focus on the important facts and features.

Good résumés have a number of features in common:

- **They list experience and education in reverse chronological order.** Whatever experience you have, you should list it in reverse chronological order, with your most recent experience or education at the top. Employers are most interested in your *recent* experience, so don't bury it at the bottom.

- **They include a professional phone number and e-mail address.** If an employer calls you, you don't really want your five-year-old sister picking up the phone and saying something embarrassing. Provide a number for a phone that *you* will answer. The embarrassment factor is key in e-mail addresses, too. Provide a professional-sounding e-mail address, not the JohnLovesStarWars@gmail.com e-mail address you created when you were in the sixth grade. You can easily get a free e-mail address from Gmail or any one of a number of other services, so set up something more professional, such as JohnSmith@gmail.com.

Home renovation programs can be a great place to learn about carpentry skills and get ideas for new projects. While most carpenters aren't particularly famous—carpentry work is usually done behind the scenes—for some lucky individuals, television has also opened up a somewhat unexpected employment avenue and created celebrity carpenters.

Bob Vila's *This Old House* launched the first celebrity carpenter.

Probably the first celebrity carpenter was Bob Vila, who hosted home-renovation show *This Old House* from 1979 to 1989. After *This Old House* ended, Vila hosted two similar shows for the next seventeen years. Vila's carpenter on *This Old House* was actually Norm Abram (and later Steve Thomas), but as the face of the show, home renovator Vila is the name people remember.

Cable TV network TLC (The Learning Channel) further popularized celebrity carpenters by featuring Ty Pennington and Carter Oosterhouse on its hit reality show *Trading Spaces*. Pennington went on to host *Extreme Makeover: Home Edition* on network television, and Oosterhouse has hosted several shows on HGTV (Home & Garden Television), including *Million Dollar Rooms*.

Finally, there are even a few kids' shows featuring main characters with at least some carpentry skills, even if they might not be called "carpenters," per se. One of the more well-known shows is *Bob the Builder* on PBS, which features Bob, a third-generation general contractor who runs a business with his business partner, Wendy, and leads a team of heavy equipment machinery in fixing various problems around the town. The show *Handy Manny*, on The Disney Channel, features Manny, a handyman with his own shop who works with his tools to make various minor repairs for his friends, family, and neighbors.

- **They list achievements concisely.** You may have a lot of achievements you want to showcase, and that's great, but do it in short bullet points. Remember that employers receive hundreds of résumés for any given job opening, so they tend to skim quickly through them. A short bulleted list of your awards and achievements will get the employer's attention; a long paragraph explaining every award in detail is likely to be overlooked.

- **They follow a logical sequence.** There are a number of ways to sequence a résumé, but you need to consider what best suits your experience and the position you're applying for. In general, carpentry is a field where experience is more useful than postsecondary education, so rather than following a format where you list your education up front, it is probably sensible to start by listing your experience. If you've earned any notable and relevant achievements, follow with those and then end with formal education. Certainly, your potential employer will want to know about your education—it just may not be of the utmost importance to him or her, so it's probably OK to put it near the end.

- **Play up your experience.** Similarly, because experience is a big part of getting a job in carpentry, you should maximize your experience. If you don't think you have much experience, then think outside the box a bit. Maybe you haven't yet worked a carpentry job, but your Eagle Scout project in high school was building new benches for the boys' locker room at the school. Or maybe you spent a summer helping your uncle renovate your grandmother's house. That's not something you'd traditionally list on a résumé, but if you find you're lacking in the experience department, you can certainly add those types of projects. The name of the game is to convince potential employers that you have enough experience or potential to be given a chance; that way, you can start gaining *real* on-the-job experience!

- **They use action-oriented language.** You want your résumé to be proactive and use powerful, action-oriented language. For example, instead of writing "Job duties included framing of doors and installation of crown molding," try "Framed doors and installed crown molding." Can you see the difference? *Framing of* and *installation of* are weaker forms of the strong verbs *frame* and *install*. Language is power, so make sure to use it to your advantage in your résumé.

- **They use language that is easy to understand.** While you want to use powerful language, you also want to be sure the words you choose are understandable. If you're applying for a job in carpentry, you can assume that your potential employer will be familiar with most general carpentry terms. But don't try to impress employers by throwing in a bunch of complicated words where plain language will do just fine. Remember that employers generally read résumés quickly—they don't have time to sit and try to figure out what you're saying. They want to know right away.

- **They are clean and free of mistakes.** This is a big one. Even when applying for a manual profession, you want to be sure your résumé is completely free of spelling and grammatical errors and inconsistencies. Nothing turns potential employers off faster than a résumé full of errors. It shows sloppiness and a lack of attention to detail—two characteristics that won't impress any potential employer.

- **They use white space.** It's tempting to try to cram as much information as possible in the one or two allotted pages for a résumé, but try to refrain from doing so. Résumés that use white space are easier to read and less likely to get tossed aside when the reader gets frustrated with trying to pore through dense blocks of text.

- **They use simple fonts and no color.** Simplicity is key in résumés. Using colors and fancy fonts tend to make them cluttered and difficult to read. It's best to stick to black and white and use a simple font. On a related note, don't use images on your résumé. It may look a little boring as text-only, but that really is preferred.

- **They are available in a universally accessible format.** You can create your résumé using any program you want, but remember that not everyone will be able to open a résumé created in, say, Apple Pages. And even if you use a more common program like Microsoft Word, the formatting can sometimes change when you e-mail it to a prospective employer. A better plan is to save your résumé in PDF format. Nearly any potential employer will be able to easily open and view a PDF, and you also ensure that your formatting stays intact.

Searching for a Job

It used to be that people looked for jobs in the newspaper. The Sunday classifieds were the place to find employment! That is rarely the case in the Information Age; nowadays, people do most of their job searching online. There are plenty of job-search engines available, such as at Monster. com, CareerBuilder.com, and Indeed.com, and it's certainly worth your time to use those.

Last but definitely not least, *never* underestimate the power of networking. When you meet anyone involved in the carpentry field, make a connection. Ask whether they have a card to give you, so you can contact them in the future. Most professionals in any industry are happy to answer any questions you have about what they do, and to give advice on reaching your career goals. Carpentry is like many other fields; often who you know is the key to your start in the industry.

Nailing the Interview

For some, interviewing is the toughest part of the job search. Résumés are always a challenge to write, but once you've got one, you only need to update it every so often. Searching for a job these days mainly involves talking to people and getting on the computer to look at job-search engines and find information about companies that are hiring in your area. But interviews … well, that's where the anxiety starts to set in. The interview is where you have to really shine if you want to get the job.

There's no absolute formula for interview success, but there are certainly some points you can consider to ready yourself for the interview process.

Dress the Part

In many careers, you want to dress up for a job interview. This is not exactly the case when you're interviewing for a carpentry position—you don't need to show up at the interview in an expensive three-piece suit. In fact, if you do, the interviewer might think you're looking for a management position rather than a carpentry position! Still, it's better to slightly overdress than to underdress. In addition to having neat, clean clothes, your appearance should also be neat and tidy.

Put on Your Interview Persona

There's really one word that should sum up your interview persona: you. Above all, you should be yourself. If you try to be someone you're not, chances are it will show. That said, you should be your *best* self.

When you bring your best self to the interview, here are some tips to help you be successful:

- **Be on time.** This should be obvious, but in case it's not: be on time! Being late to an interview leaves a poor first impression.
- **Relax!** Anxiety is your biggest enemy in an interview. If you can't relax, it'll show, and your interview won't be as successful as you'd like it to be.

- **Be confident.** Have faith in your skills. This is your life's vocation: carpentry! It's something you love to do, and you're good at it. If you weren't, you wouldn't be devoting your career to it. So have confidence in yourself. Even if you don't have much experience yet, you still have ability.

- **Be humble.** Sounds contrary, right? I just told you to be confident. Well, you need to be confident *and* humble. Nobody likes a braggart. You can be confident in your skills as a carpenter but still have humility. The trick is to answer questions honestly and confidently, but not to go overboard boasting about your accomplishments or abilities.

- **Listen.** The potential employer isn't just interviewing you, you're also interviewing them. Listen to what they are saying and you will learn a lot. Interviewers will often start by telling you about their company, and then they'll ask you questions about what you're looking for in a job. If you can use some of what they said about their company in your answer, it will show that you were interested in the company, and it will make the interviewer look favorably on you as a candidate. Little things like that make a difference in an interview.

- **Use good posture.** Sit up straight! Slouching can communicate boredom or laziness—and that's the last thing you want a potential employer to think about you, particularly for a carpentry job!

- **Smile!** It's amazing the difference a smile can make. Make a point to smile periodically during the interview.

- **Prepare some questions.** It's common for interviewers to ask you if you have any questions when the interview ends. Have a few ready to ask. This shows you're interested in the job. If you have no questions, the interviewer may interpret that as a lack of interest in the position.

- **Thank the interviewer.** When the interview is finished, shake the interviewer's hand and thank him or her. Send a thank-you e-mail the day after the interview, thanking the interviewer for their time and expressing your interest in the job. You can also encourage them to contact you if they have any further questions.

Be Ready for Questions

Many of the questions you'll be asked during an interview for a carpentry job are likely the same types of questions you'd be asked for *any* job interview, such as:

- Please share your greatest strengths and weaknesses.
- What are your career goals?
- Why did you leave your last job?
- What are you looking for in a job?
- What do you know about our organization?
- Why should we hire you?

Be honest when you answer these questions. If you try to answer what you *think* the interviewer wants to hear, you'll just end up sounding awkward. It's always better to just be honest.

It's likely that in addition to general questions, you'll also be asked questions specific to your knowledge of the field of carpentry. You might be asked situational questions, such as, "What would you do if you discovered that your coworker was violating the building code?" or "How do you clean and maintain your tools after use?" You might also be asked questions about hierarchy on a jobsite, such as, "What do you see as the role of an apprentice?" Particularly because there are safety issues involved in the field of construction and carpentry, it's important that everyone on a jobsite respects the position of others on the crew.

You may also be asked safety-related questions. Carpentry can be a dangerous field since you're working with power tools and sometimes at high elevations.

Taking appropriate safety measures is key in the field of carpentry.

Workplace accidents can and do happen; however, employers should have safety procedures in place to protect their employees from on-the-job hazards. Whether you are interviewing for a summer job or an apprenticeship, always ask questions to ensure any potential employer has a solid reputation for providing a safe workplace.

Ready to Get Started?

Now you've read an entire book about becoming a carpenter. Are you interested? Inspired? Wondering what the next step is?

The next step is to get out there and start building! Find some small projects and try your hand at them. But wait—you'll need tools to do it. If you visit your local hardware store, you'll be faced with aisles upon aisles of tools, and you might wonder where to start. So here's a list of some essential tools if you want to start getting busy with some carpentry projects:

- **A tool belt**. This one should go without saying. If you don't have a tool belt, you don't really have any way to carry your hand tools. You could put them in a toolbox, of course, but lugging around a heavy toolbox isn't terribly practical. Better to invest in a good tool belt so you can have just the tools you need at hand for any given project.
- **Hand tools**. These include a hammer, screwdrivers, a tape measure, a carpenter's pencil and a chalk line,

a utility knife, a nail puller, levels, a chisel, tin snips, and a speed square.

- **Power tools**. You could do everything by hand, but power tools can make any job much easier. The must-have power tools when you're starting out include a circular saw, a power drill, a reciprocating saw, and an extension cord.

- **Extras**. These aren't must-haves; rather, they're "nice-to-haves." They include an air compressor, a nail gun, an air hose, a table saw, and a compound miter saw. Also, you might need items like files or rasps, vices, clamps, ladders, sawhorses, or shovels, depending on the job. And don't forget safety goggles, gloves, and sturdy shoes!

You can always start small, too. Grab a hammer, a couple of screwdrivers, a saw, and some nails and screws, and go to town. You might not even need a permanent workbench in your garage—today hardware stores sell portable or folding workbenches of various sizes and durability.

And don't forget, you can always buy used tools; there's no need to spend a fortune on brand-new tools. Check garage and estate sales in your area—as people age and are no longer interested in or able to take on carpentry projects, they often sell their extra tools. You can also search online at shopping sites like eBay or Craigslist for good prices on used tools. Be sure to speak with your parents before making any purchases on the Internet.

What sorts of projects might be waiting for you at home? You could put some shelves up in your garage, put up a new mantel over your fireplace, rebuild the gate leading into your backyard, or repair and refinish the old dresser that your neighbor convinced your family to take when they moved. Ask your parents if they have any projects they will let you practice on. You never know what's been lurking on their to-do list and they just haven't had time to get to it.

So, what are you waiting for? Grab your hammer and get to it!

Glossary

3-D printing Creating an object from a three-dimensional digital model. This process usually involves laying down many thin layers of a building material.

accredit To recognize an educational institution as maintaining standards that qualify the graduates for admission to higher or more specialized institutions or for professional practice.

apprenticeship A position where a person new to a field works under a more experienced person to learn the trade.

artisanal Describing something that is produced in limited quantities, often using traditional methods.

blueprint A technical design plan.

board feet A specialized unit of quantity for lumber equal to the volume of a board 12 × 12 × 1 inches (30.5 × 30.5 × 2.54 centimeters).

CADD Stands for computer-aided drafting and design; a type of software that allows designers to create plans for structures.

dexterity Skill at performing tasks with the hands.

entrepreneur A person who creates, organizes, and operates a business.

expat Short for expatriate, an expat is a person who lives outside of his or her native country.

hardwood A type of wood sourced from a broad-leafed tree species.

hermetically A process of sealing something so it is completely airtight.

historic integrity The state of being consistent with a particular time period.

journeyman A trained worker. In carpentry, a journeyman has more experience than an apprentice but less than a master carpenter.

MBE Stands for minority business enterprise and refers to a company at least 51 percent owned and/or operated by a socially or economically disadvantaged person.

median The midpoint of a distribution of values.

Neolithic Relating to the later part of the Stone Age.

prefabricate To manufacture the parts of something beforehand so that it can be later built by assembling the parts together.

reclaimed Recovered for reuse or recycled.

RFP Stands for request for proposals. Businesses put out an RFP when they are looking for contractors to do a job.

softwood A type of wood sourced from coniferous tree species.

sustainability Involving methods that do not completely use up or destroy natural resources.

union An organization of workers formed to protect those workers' rights.

urban sprawl Uncontrolled expansion of an urban area.

visual-spatial The ability to mentally manipulate objects.

WBE Stands for woman business enterprise and refers to a company where a woman owns and controls at least 51 percent of the business.

Further Information

Books

Carlsen, Spike. *The Backyard Homestead Book of Building Projects.* North Adams, MA: Storey Publishing, 2014.

Cory, Steve. *Outdoor Wood Projects: 24 Projects You Can Build in a Weekend.* Newtown, CT: Taunton Press, 2014.

Thiel, David, ed. *I Can Do That! Woodworking Projects: Updated & Expanded.* Cincinnati: Popular Woodworking Books, 2012.

Websites

Habitat for Humanity
www.habitat.org
If you want to get some experience in building, Habitat for Humanity is an excellent place to start. They have volunteer opportunities worldwide.

Hammerstone School
www.hammerstoneschool.com
If you're a female interested in pursuing a career in carpentry, you may be interested in the classes offered by the Hammerstone School.

United Brotherhood of Carpenters and Joiners of America
www.carpenters.org/Home.aspx
This website is for the largest carpenters' union in the United States, and it is full of useful information about training and skills needed to succeed in the field.

Bibliography

Amoia, Steve. "Journeyman Carpenter Job Description." *Global Post*. n.d. http://everydaylife.globalpost.com/journeyman-carpenter-job-description-2373.html.

Art Directory. "Marcus Vitruvius Pollio." http://www.vitruvius-pollio.com.

Brown, Tara Tiger. "The Death of Shop Class and America's Skilled Workforce." Forbes.com. May 30, 2012. http://www.forbes.com/sites/tarabrown/2012/05/30/the-death-of-shop-class-and-americas-high-skilled-workforce.

Bureau of Labor Statistics, US Department of Labor, *Occupational Outlook Handbook*, 2014-15 Edition, Carpenters. Accessed June 5, 2015. http://www.bls.gov/ooh/construction-and-extraction/carpenters.htm.

Bureau of Labor Statistics, US Department of Labor, *Occupational Outlook Handbook*, 2014-15 Edition, Woodworkers. Accessed May 31, 2015. http://www.bls.gov/ooh/production/woodworkers.htm.

"Carpenter: Salary" *U.S. News & World Report*. n.d. http://money.usnews.com/careers/best-jobs/carpenter/salary.

"Carpenters – The Life of a Carpenter." n.d. http://www.carpenterlane.com.

"Carpentry." National Center for Construction Education and Research. n.d. http://www.nccer.org/carpentry.

"Carpentry Certification and Licensure Programs." Study.com. n.d. http://study.com/articles/Carpentry_Certification_and_Licensure_Programs.html.

"Certified Lead Carpenter (CLC)." National Association of the Remodeling Industry. n.d. http://www.nari.org/industry/development/certification/certified-lead-carpenter-clc.

Cuneo, Eileen Colkin. "What to Expect with Reclaimed Wood." This Old House. n.d. http://www.thisoldhouse.com/toh/article/0,,1606344,00.html.

Esler, Bill. "3D Printed Wood Application Uses Granular Wood Flour." Woodworking Network. Accessed June 5, 2015. http://www.woodworkingnetwork.com/wood/components-sourcing/3d-printed-wood-application-uses-granular-wood-flour.

"Evidence From Census 2000 About Earnings by Detailed Occupation for Men and Women." May 2004. http://www.census.gov/prod/2004pubs/censr-15.pdf.

"Fun Forest Facts." The Forest Foundation. n.d. http://www.calforestfoundation.org/Students-And-Teachers/Fun-Forest-Facts.htm.

Gabr, Ahmed. "Egypt's Most Famous Female Carpenter Is Breaking the Mold to Build a Global Brand." Wamda. November 4, 2013. http://www.wamda.com/2013/11/egypt-s-most-famous-female-carpenter-is-breaking-the-mold-to-build-a-global-brand.

Koenig, Karen. "UK Designer Grows Complete Furniture Pieces." Woodworking Network. Accessed June 2, 2015. http://www.woodworkingnetwork.com/furniture/uk-designer-grows-complete-furniture-pieces.

Locsin, Aurelio. "Do You Need to Have Certification to Be a Carpenter?" *Houston Chronicle.* n.d. http://work.chron.com/need-certification-carpenter-14947.html.

Lundahl, Erika. "Less Than 2 Percent of Carpenters Are Women—Meet the Master Builder Working to Change That." *Yes!* September 26, 2013. http://www.yesmagazine.org/new-economy/less-than-two-percent-of-carpenters-are-women-meet-master-builder.

"Online Carpentry Certificates and Certification Programs." Study.com. n.d. http://study.com/articles/Online_Carpentry_Certificates_and_Certification_Programs.html#relatedSchoolsList.

"OSH Answers Fact Sheets." Canadian Centre for Occupational Health and Safety. n.d. http://www.ccohs.ca/oshanswers/occup_workplace/carpenter.html.

Prigg, Mark. "The First Carpenters? 7,000 Year Old German Water Wells Found to Be Earliest Use of Wood for Construction." *Daily Mail.* http://www.dailymail.co.uk/sciencetech/article-2255383/The-carpenters-7-000-year-old-German-water-wells-reveal-earliest-known-use-wood-construction.html.

Sharkey, Joe. "The School Bell Tolls for Shop Class." *The New York Times.* June 30, 1996. http://www.nytimes.com/1996/06/30/nyregion/the-school-bell-tolls-for-shop-class.html.

Shpak, Scott. "Highest-Paid Union Carpenters." *Houston Chronicle.* n.d. http://work.chron.com/highestpaid-union-carpenters-30422.html.

Taylor, Glenda. "Essential Responsibilities of a Union Carpenter." *Houston Chronicle*. n.d. http://work.chron.com/essential-responsibilities-union-carpenter-21109.html.

Tucker, Christine. "Situational Interview Questions for a Carpentry Helper." *Houston Chronicle*. n.d. http://work.chron.com/situational-interview-questions-carpentry-helper-25465.html.

Viegas, Jennifer. "Tool Use by Early Humans Started Much Earlier." Discovery News. November 27, 2012. http://news.discovery.com/history/archaeology/early-human-tool-use.htm.

Index

Page numbers in **boldface** are illustrations. Entries in **boldface** are glossary terms.

About the Author

Cathleen Small is an editor and author who has written numerous books for Cavendish Square Publishing. She recently tested her own carpentry skills in the fixer-upper house she bought with her husband and quickly decided she should stick to writing about carpentry and leave the hands-on work to the pros. When she's not botching home-improvement projects, Cathleen enjoys hanging out with her two sons and two pugs in the San Francisco Bay Area.